# LAWREN HARRIS
## CONTRASTS:
### In the Ward

# LAWREN HARRIS
## CONTRASTS:
### In the Ward

A BOOK OF POETRY AND PAINTINGS

Edited and Introduced by Gregory Betts

EXILE
editions

Fiction Poetry Translation Drama and Nonfiction

Library and Archives Canada Cataloguing in Publication

Harris, Lawren, 1885-1970
    Lawren Harris : contrasts : in the ward -- a book of poetry and paintings / Lawren Harris ; Gregory Betts, editor/ introduction.

(Exile classic series ; 26)
Includes bibliographical references.
ISBN 978-1-55096-308-3

    1. Toronto (Ont.)--History--20th century--Poetry.  2. Toronto (Ont.)--History--20th century--Pictorial works.
I. Betts, Gregory, 1975-  II. Title.  III. Series: Exile classics ; 26

PS8515.A7893I5 2012          C811'.52          C2012-905473-9

Design and Composition by Steamroller Ascension~mc
Typeset in the Akzidenz Grotesk, Bembo, Book Antiqua, Garamond, and Stone fonts at the Moons of Jupiter Studios
Printed by Imprimerie Gauvin

Published by Exile Editions Ltd ~ www.ExileEditions.com
144483 Southgate Road 14 – GD, Holstein ON, N0G 2A0
Printed and bound in Canada in 2012

The publisher would like to acknowledge the financial support of the Canada Council for the Arts, the Government of Canada through the Canada Book Fund (CBF), the Ontario Arts Council, and the Ontario Media Development Corporation, for our publishing activities.

Canadian Sales: The Canadian Manda Group, 165 Dufferin Street, Toronto ON  M6K 3H6
www.mandagroup.com     416 516 0911

North American and international Distribution, and U.S. Sales:
Independent Publishers Group, 814 North Franklin Street, Chicago IL  60610
www.ipgbook.com     toll free: 1 800 888 4741

*this book is dedicated to*

**Diane Betts**

# CONTENTS

## THE PAINTINGS

The paintings reproduced on the pages noted above are details of the originals. Please see page 140 for full images and descriptions of the paintings, and where they are located. (in order of appearance).

## *Acknowledgements*

I would like to thank the following people for their help with this project, without whom it most certainly could not have been realized: Ray Ellenwood, Stewart Sheppard, Andrea Dixon, rob mclennan, Glenn Willmott, Rosemary Hale, Janine Butler, Barry Callaghan, Michael Callaghan, John Lennox, Donald Rance, and of course Exile Editions. The following archives, galleries, and collections were consulted: the Art Gallery of Ontario, the National Gallery, the McMichael Gallery, the Robert McLaughlin Gallery, the Archives of the Arts and Letters Club, Thomas Fischer Rare Books Library, McMaster Special Collections, the Clara Thomas Special Collections at York University, the National Gallery of Canada, and, of course, Library and Archives Canada. Writings by Joan Murray, Charles Hill, Dennis Reid, Jeremy Adamson, Ann Davis, and Andrew Hunter were essential in advancing the conceptual frame of the project. Funding for the research was generously provided by the Social Science Humanities Research Council and Brock University's Humanities Research Institute. Perhaps most importantly of all, the following people provided key interest, support, and feedback for the project over glasses of wine, coffee, and tea which made it all seem worthwhile throughout its gestation phase: Colin Hill, Clelia Scala, Nathalie Foy, Peter Wilson, Keith Inman, Jordan Scott, James Depew, Dean Irvine, Max Middle, Andrew Porteus, Nicole Anderson, and Brian Trehearne. Nothing in my life is possible without Lisa R. Betts, so full thanks and endless gratitude belong to her.

# INTRODUCTION

Before Lawren Harris created and led the Group of Seven into the national spotlight in the 1920s, he started here, in the Ward. Standing in the doorway of the prestigious Arts and Letters Club, probably after an extended lunch, staring down a long stretch of mud road that led into the Ward – also sometimes known as St. John's Shtetl. If there was a mystery to the city in those days, a secret place that combined danger and culture, song and decrepitude, here it was. Disaccommodated Jewish and Italian immigrants had arrived en masse in Canada between 1900 and 1914 – nearly 100,000 Jews immigrated to the country during this period alone (Powell 165), while the Italian population in Toronto tripled (Baily 231). They collected in Toronto's decrepit Ward district and infused it with their songs, food, and culture: in this mixed residential, commercial, and open-air market community, the Old World claimed its inauspicious presence

in the New. Harris could stand on the step of his cushy bourgeois respite and stare long into the mystery of poverty. He was no stranger to exotic adventures: in 1909 he had travelled as illustrator with the writer Norman Duncan on camelback from Beersheba to Damascus on assignment for *Harper's Magazine* (published in issues 117 and 118). But this was different; this was an adventure in his own country, his own city, on the very edge of his own life. Before the Group of Seven set off on their nationalist-cum-romantic adventures into the heart of the Canadian wilderness, before Bertram Brooker pushed Canadian modernism into the avant-garde, Harris confronted the cold underbelly of the city of Toronto – he left the club and entered the untouched, untamed place in its imagination. It was a question he set off searching for; a question concerning the meaning of the metaphor of the poverty that lay before him:

*Are you sad when you look down city lanes,*
*Lanes littered with ashes, boxes, cans, old rags;*
*Dirty, musty, garbage-reeking lanes*
*Behind the soot-dripped backs of blunt houses,*
*Sour yards and slack-sagging fences?*
("A Question")

The question was not just one of buildings and architecture, but of the fact of living in such conditions – of an existence and a spirit shaped by such surroundings:

*When you see great cities,*
*Jagged squares of baked clay, and steel and stone,*
*Canals of filth under every street,*
*Smoke-breathed, din-shrouded,*
*Seething with blind, driven people –*
*Seeing pilgrims settling down in the earth's scum,*
*In mud,*
*Feeling swine,*
*Are you sad?*
*Are you like that?*

It was the thought that the people in the Ward were "Outcast from beauty, / Even afraid of beauty" that made it all seem terrible and meaningful.

In these paintings in this book, produced primarily before but also concurrent with the formation of the Group of Seven, we have one of the earliest glimpses of urban poverty in Canada. It took a modernist, someone Northrop Frye declared "Canada's only important revolutionary painter" (*Northrop* 85), to want to look. The dirt streets, the dishevelled shacks, the broken shutters. The warped homes possess a weariness, jutting out from loping hills more out of stoic habit than fierce, defiant determination. In another context, Frye notes "the ironic eye of a potentially abstract painter has caught, not the pictorial essence of the building, but, on the contrary, the sense of its pictorial incongruity. The buildings have proportions, so he leaves them imprisoned in their own angularity" ("The Pursuit" 54). The paintings are not typical of the work that turned the Group of Seven into a national phenomenon. They are not akin to the inhuman beauty of the lonely Jack Pines sculpted by fierce north winds. But these paintings are also powerful and emotive representations of a lost time and place in Torontonian and

Canadian history. Those familiar with Harris' later work will notice the early fascination with sharply defined geometrical objects. As with his landscapes and abstractions, Harris' cityscapes are consistently depopulated – even the people that do appear are blurred into figurative objects: at one with the abstracted surroundings. They are often little more than convenient places for a dash of contrasting colour.

The poems, however, produced at the same time as the urban canvases, populate the barren city. They are the figures detached from the ground depicted in the canvases: the freely moving Time separated from the constrained Space of the paintings. The voices and looks and imprints of inhabitants shape these poems as Harris wanders the urban streets with curiosity and open wonder. True, the speaker in the poems meanders through abstractions and ideologies, but the grime and litter are given their own voice throughout these poems. Even the buildings are anthropomorphized in the poems: in "A Note of Colour," the narrator marvels at a painted red door that "smiles, and even laughs" in the face of the antipodal "bleary with grime, and bulging, filthy" surroundings. Like the paintings, these jangly poems are also imprisoned in their own angularity that well suits their subject.

Like so many of the poems, "Morning and Evening" is a carefully constructed study in contrasts. Structurally, the first six lines of each stanza establish the opposite moods of the workers going to and returning from their daily toil: optimistic in the morning and then dispirited at night. The verbatim repetition of lines 8 through 11 in the second stanza stabilizes the constant city through which the workers move. The streetcars rattle and clang the same both morning and night, though the sound in the ears of the people changes. A further contrast emerges in this poem: Harris reveals himself at odds with the working class. Morning and night, he walks "Through the crowds," against the crowds, to observe their expressions, rather than walking *with* the crowds as a fellow worker. Of course, the wealthy, property-owning Harris was a tourist in the working-class neighbourhoods of Toronto, discovering the features and idiosyncrasies of a world not his own: witnessing the dispirited walk home after a long day working in factories like those owned by his parents. Critics of his day only heard the difference of these poems from the inherited models of poetry Canadians at the time preferred. These models all depended on prettiness or preciousness of phrase. Harris' critics never paused to consider how his difference from that model points towards a new form and a new style. For instance, his flat tone captures the meanness, ugliness, and plainness of quotidian life in the Ward. Rather than seek epiphany in these details, they are positioned as objective obstacles to his spiritual quest.

The depopulated paintings do something similar in their representation of Space. Harris abstracts the functional dwelling places from the people who live in them. Furthermore, the geometrical patterning of the canvases portrays the Ward not as a functioning, even colourful, neighbourhood in the present, but as a timeless realm of decayed objects. These are not real houses, as much as platonic abstractions of poor, rundown houses – they destabilize or rather, in the modernist vocabulary of Schlovsky and Stein, *defamiliarize* Toronto's streets. By this subtle alteration, the paintings indicate Harris' occultist conviction that Space and the material present are determined by convention and perception rather than through absolute presence. Harris would eventually perfect this defamiliarization technique in his more blatantly spiritualized mountain and iceberg landscapes. At this point in his career, however, Harris was content exploring the isolation of figures and grounds abstracted into separate media.

In his notebooks from the period, he acknowledges the struggle of workers to alleviate their crushing  experience of exploitation, but confesses his abstraction from poverty and the vortex of human affairs: "When labour, the workers are ready to take over the machine that capital has built (labour built it equally) then they will take over the machine and run it, perhaps better, certainly to the greater good of the greater number. But…. We are forever advancing by replacing one delusion by another which is nearer the truth, yet a delusion nevertheless. Each delusion that we chase or adhere to seems the great remedy, the panacea, the solution, but it is not. Once it is put into practice we get another idea; chase another delusion. Always progress in the long run of course but nevertheless delusions." (Notebook 2-5). These lines convey both his dissatisfaction with the poverty of human life and spirit, but also his overarching optimism. Evidence of both is apparent in all the work collected here.

With these interconnected themes informing their production, the poetry and paintings complement each other. Reconnecting them here for the first time by restaging them side by side, suggests an optimism that figure and ground could be realigned, made spiritually unified despite a fractured, war-torn world. Harris was a famous optimist, even despite the modernist malaise, and set his vision within a bigger picture beyond the transitory problems of day-to-day life. As he writes:

*Girls go wrong,*
*Wars come along.*
*The victorious get nothing.*
*The conquered get nothing.*

*Nobody gets anything.*
*Everyone is defeated*
*But never beaten. –*
*People are all right.*
  ("People Are All Right")

The paradoxically cynical-optimism of these lines suggests the personal struggle and transformation Harris had undergone during his urban period. Though born into one of the wealthiest families in the Dominion, the protective bubble that kept him shrouded from the world burst with the death of his great friend Tom Thompson in 1917 and of his brother Howard in 1918. Though well into his adulthood, this sudden confrontation with death deeply shocked the painter. He suffered a nervous breakdown and was discharged from his position as a lieutenant in the Tenth Royal Grenadier Regiment (where he designed targets resembling German architecture and uniforms), and retreated to the family summer home (see Larisey 34-36 for more). Nervous and agitated from the loss, Harris nevertheless began to confront the reality of life beyond the idyllic protection of his parents' wealth.

Painting became ever more significant in his investigation of life, death, and what he would later describe as the "spiritual realities" of the world. The change in his perception is apparent in the urban paintings that emerged: the paintings in this book generally lack the prettiness, the tidiness, and the decorum of his first urban works. Life was suddenly at stake in every part of the world surrounding him. His spiritual intensity ultimately led him from the urban theme to new subjects, including the widely celebrated spiritualized wilderness paintings and eventually, after he fled Toronto in 1934, to mystical abstractions. His first project, now recast here, was to explore and document the degradations and spiritual potential of his urban home – to picture his crumbling world fragmented in Time and Space, with the thinly veiled hope of cosmic reunion.

Editor's notes ~ *Contrasts: A Book of Verse by Lawren Harris* was originally published by McClelland & Stewart in Toronto in 1922. The spelling, punctuation and grammar used by Lawren Harris have been retained to respect the original presentation. And a special thank you to Stewart Sheppard and the Estate of Lawren Harris for the kind permission, as granted to Exile Editions in 2012, to reproducce all of the artwork as presented herein.

Lawren Stewart Harris, 1885–1970

*taken by Bess Housser,*
*in Santa Fe, New Mexico, c.1939*

It appears from all turbulent signs that we move now into
a new order, perhaps into the rule of workers of the world
and whatever system they, in the process of taking over power,
devise. That is good. For the extrication of society from
the fabric of the intellectually indefensible system of private
capitalism into something more equitable and with less emphasis
on mere shrewdness and money-grubbing and exploitation can
mean a thousand benefits.

The interdependence of all men, all peoples, everywhere,
throughout time, is epitomized in every great creative work of art.

— LAWREN HARRIS, *The Creative Individual and A New Order*

# I

# DESCRIPTIVE

## A Note of Colour

In a part of the city that is ever shrouded in sooty smoke,
and amid huge, hard buildings, hides a gloomy house of
broken grey rough-cast, like a sickly sin in a callous soul.

Streams of wires run by it wailing in the murky wind.
Two half dead chestnut trees, black and broken, stand
wearily before it, subdued by a bare rigid telephone pole.

The windows are bleary with grime, and bulging, filthy
rags plug the broken panes.

Torn blinds of cold judas green chill whatever light
sifts through the smoky air.

Dirty shutters sag this way and that like dancers
suddenly stopped in an aimless movement.

But the street door smiles, and even laughs, when the
hazy sunlight falls on it —

Someone had painted it a bright gay red.

## In a Tea Room

The thin, pale, flat breasted girl
Gazes out of the window
Up to the sky,
To the big, round, white billows of clouds
As they float across the fresh blue —
Her eyes look up,
And she smiles a wistful, longing smile.

The red-headed, round, white-rosy young thing
Who brings her tea
Looks out of the window
Down at the street,
At the big-voiced, jaunty young men
As they swagger past —
She glances down
And smiles a saucy, knowing smile.

## The Evangelist

A guy on the street corner
Shouts Christ at the crowd,
And the passers by
Glance and smile,
Or shrug a shoulder,
And look away —
Bums loiter on the curbs
Like flies indifferent of feeding,
Chew tobacco, smoke, spit
And gaze at the girls —
Behind a row of opened windows,
In a pool room
A crowd of young fellows
In shirt sleeves
Lean over the tables
And whack the balls around —
Across the street
In a flashy store
A hoarse auctioneer
Sells bogus jewellery to gawky men —
Motors bleat past,
Street cars stop,
Spill out people,

Take on people
And start again,
And the guy
On the street corner
Shouts Christ at the crowd.

## Morning and Evening

Bathed in the morning sun I walk up street
Through the crowds swarming to the daily grind.
The air is fresh and cool.
Everyone is alert and ready for the day's grind.
People are friendly, and smile, and give how-d'you-do's
    and how-are-you's easily.
They enjoy their fellows and the lilt of the morning.
The rattle and clanging of street cars, the roar of
    heavily laden trucks, the piercing bleat of arrogant
    motor horns — all discordant noises of
    the street
Bespeak to them the romantic import of human affairs.
Facing the morning sun people swarm to the daily grind.

Towards evening I walk down street
Through the crowds returning from the daily grind.
The air is stale and heavy.
Everyone is weary and hurries homeward, intent on rest.
People are occupied with themselves and salute one
    another grudgingly, or not at all.
They have nothing for their fellows.

The rattle and clanging of street cars, the roar of
    heavily laden trucks, the piercing bleat of arrogant
    motor horns—all the discordant noises of
    the street
Bespeak to them the jangle and futility of human affairs.
Facing homewards, people swarm from the daily grind.

## The Harbour

Here in the harbour the big ships are so still.
Only the little boats ply to and fro,
Darting over their tiny, confined surface
Like silly water beetles.
And on shore, in the town, cars clatter along the streets,
Harshly grumble as they gather speed, squeal around
    the curves, scrunch as they stop.
And horse hooves pock-pock on the hard pavement.
Motor horns shriek along every thoroughfare, piercingly
    brazen.
Drays and trucks rumble by, bang over the car tracks,
    scrape against the curbs,
And along the streets, and across the streets at all angles,
And in and out of buildings
Men hurry, impatient and preoccupied —
And beyond lies the sea.

Here in the harbour
All is fretful, pained activity.
All the noises are whining, grinding, shrill.
Everything is sick, sore and bruised.
Men are on petty days —

Are evil, lewd, bad-breathed —
Men head their ships to the harbour,
Crave to get to the harbour,
But the harbour is no haven for men.

## Little Houses

Dreamers ever leave you, little houses
While you doze the long days away
In snug little villages and on easy hillsides,
Along lazy rivers and in sleepy valleys —
Little houses tucked in little yards
Behind low, white fences or bushy green hedges,
Behind old apple trees and syringa bushes,
Or under big elms —
Plump, well fed, clean little houses,
A big, round rain barrel by the side door,
Old-lady-like front porches, and fat rear porches,
And full woodsheds —
Lots of wood for the winter,
For the kitchen range and the big base burner in the sitting room —
Homes for contented folks,
Easy-going, fruit-preserving, cookie-making folks
The dreamers ever leave you —
They hear a vague, far cry,
Perhaps the call of some vacant, high place,
So often only the wailing of a beckoning pain,
But the dreamers ever leave you.

## Greetings

The other day
Walking along the street
I heard a man singing
High in the air
Above my head —
I looked up
And saw a lineman
Atop a telephone pole
Spiking on cross ties
To the rhythm of his song —
I smiled and said
"That's the stuff"
And he smiled back
And told me
To go to hell
As a man will
When he understands another.

## Picnic Grounds

Old, littered picnic grounds,
Scraps of greasy, jammy paper about,
And stale crusts, and shrivelling orange peels and
    banana skins turning to a rich walnut colour.
Worn ground, sodden and sour with soda water and
    pop; tea, coffee and milk,
And egg shells in the grass like broken mushrooms.
Garbage of frivol,
Of people going to the open to eat and be gay,
And leaving a litter behind.
Stale joys and fading laughter lingering in the air,
Stolen kisses and sly hugs, giggles and guffaws,
Cajolings, blushes and lost virginities —
O, the whole earth where men live
Is like old, stale, picnic grounds,
Robbed of freshness,
Raped of sweetness,
Dying ever so slowly through the ages.

## Overlooking the Sea

The sea doesn't amount to much when you're not on it.
It just lies out there,
A surface for ships to sail over
From one bit of land to another.
Cockle shells they are, full of stuff, sailing great distances,
    so it seems to them.
But they don't amount to much.
It's true, they are very solemn and majestic when you are
    under their bows.
But so are ant hills when your head is low in the grass.
No, from this hill, the sea doesn't look to be anything
    much.
Just a flat puddle of water, wind-brushed to a deep blue,
And a sharp drawn line where it meets the sky.
Of course, I know it takes days and days to sail across the
    sea.
But that's nothing.
Days pass quickly.
Morning, noon and night.
And then another day.

Now, if it took a million years to cross the sea,
It might be something to talk about.
But even a million years will pass away,
And when they are gone, and done with,
It wouldn't be anything to wonder at, either.
Not that I don't love the sea. I do.
It makes a fine background for men,
And I admit that ships are wonderful toys, so ingenious
        and beautiful, often inspiring.
And everything that has to do with ships and shipping is
        so alluring —
Breakwaters, quays and docks,
Ship chandlers, sail lofts, derricks and winches.
And light houses on the very end of capes and far out to
        sea on rocks.
And bell buoys and whistling buoys.
And busy little harbour tugs.
O, the sea has a great call for men,
Because it is so peaceful, I suppose.
The same flat stretches day after day.
Even in great storms it is very peaceful, very restful.
Perhaps most restful in great storms.
Its waves roll with ceaseless rhythm and are such little things.

Nothing like so large, comparatively, as the waves tugs
make in harbours.
No really, the sea doesn't amount to much when you're not
on it.

## City Heat

The streets are hot under the sun,
Surging with animal heat,
Sucked to the surface
Through pores, through angers, through feverishness
By the sun.

The heat jiggles along every street,
Reverberates from the scorching pavement,
Hot brick walls, stone walls and side walks —
Runs everywhere
With licking-hot, laughing tongues
Driven by the sun.

The breezes are dead,
Only the slow undulating coarse stench
From hot meals, dead meats,
Stinking steam, sour milk
And sour sweat
Moves —
Soughing swamp breathings
In the pestilential city.

Babies in the heat,
The sick in the heat,
Pain in the heat,
Noises running the waves of heat,
Metal-hot, nasal noises,
Cryings, bawlings, clangings
And wearied voices
Ringing in the head
Like the close-singing remoteness
Of delirium.

From out the city
Oozes forth
A sticky, cloying, stinking thickness,
Sucked to the surface
By the sun.

In the Ward, 1920

Eaton Manufacturing Building, 1911

Hurdy Gurdy, 1913

Houses, Chestnut Street, 1919

# II

# EMOTIONAL

## You and I, Friend

Let us, you and I, friend, take off our disguise and
    rest awhile —
Let us unmask —
We need no longer assert our little selves — no longer
    insult one another.
You and I have no need of doing so —
Let us not accentuate each our bias, nor parade our
    opinions, nor any of our store of learning —
Let us rid ourselves of our conceits, our beliefs, and
    prejudices and our poor, foolish fears —
We have nothing to fear —
We need not fear beauty — the hidden, precious things
    that support us —
We need not be ashamed of our deep desire to hold
    and sustain all men —
Nor need we hide the majestic region in the heart
    where great souls meet —
For these are not our own —
We know that we are empty handed, —
There is no longer any need of pretense —
We are strong enough to dispense with that —
So, let us, you and I, friend, take off our disguise
And rest awhile.

## After War

Pain dust
Settling on the earth
After storm-stirrings—
Quietly settling
In slow sorrows.

## Who Are You?

Who are you
With such beautiful pools of pain behind your eyes,
Such gentle smiles?
You look out on men
From the depths of your pain
And so often see only what hurts,
And so you return to your silent pools —
Ever with gifts.

## Drops of Pain

I seek the life's blood of every pleasure.
The age-long, tediously distilled drops of pain.
They would elude me,
So chaste, so shy, so lovely,
So careful of their hallowed beauty.
Forever they retreat with their gifts,
Leaving behind only bitterness
To confuse the faint hearted.
Yet, they live only to give,
Seeking fulfillment
In great lovers.

## The Age

This is the age of the soul's degradation,
Of tossing into the sun's light
The dross and slime of life,
And glorying in the miserable glitter.
Hell's tinsel, and allurements and stupifying glare
Shot over the soul's great sadness
With cries and sneers and hard hosannahs.

## What a World!

What a world!
Buzzing through space like some hurt bee
Enwrapped, gloomed and hugged in pain —
Idiot world, jay world,
Little speck of a world —
Millions of men on it
Striving, struggling.
Building up, tearing down and grubbing in it,
Leaving no stone unturned —
Mad, sad, craving men
Seeking riches everywhere, anyhow, at all times —
What a world!
Great, heroic little world,
Riding the heavens
Through hell to glory
With its mad, seething cargo.

## Pity the Vindictive

Pity the vindictive
Living in the nerves of their snapping teeth,
Tearing at their own unhealing wounds
Resentful of beautifully smooth, white skin—
Warm in snarls,
Loving in hate,
Living in lust,
Alive, only in the raw—
O, pity the poor, far-alienated,
Torn bleeding from men
By the beast.

## Good Fellows

There is a fake brotherliness
Drummed up by booze —
Good fellows
On a shot
Or two
Of hooch —
Getting together to souse,
Babbling, back slapping,
Stuttering, spluttering,
Lolling on each other,
Differences drowned —
Pickled to the gills,
Parboiled, plastered,
Good Fellows
Drooling slime words
From loose lips —
Women
Made whores,
Dragged through dirt
And exhibited —
"Here's to the ladies,
Let joy be unrefined."

## Keep Moving

Don't settle down —
Just as sure
As you get yourself
All fixed
And snug
Something
Will come along
And bump you out —
Keep on moving,
And when you rest,
Keep an eye
Open, knowing
You won't be
Where you are
For long —
Just be ready
To hump yourself —
Life has a sheaf
Of itches and pin pricks,
Slow aches and surprises,
Hard pangs and soft pains —
Cures for all comfort.

## Rehearsal

Come join the self-elected martyrs, the fake downtrodden.
They who isolate themselves
To find a distinction, a different taste, a petty enhancement.
Load yourself with melancholy burdens.
Build up a world of sadness, and beauty
That has flown from majesty —
Beauty that is puny and wan,
And slowly starves in its own drab wilderness
With only itself to feed upon.
Fill yourself with heavy tales.
Affect wounded looks,
Chastise, scourge, torture yourself.
Fondle your false greatness,
Cherish your foolish loneliness,
Listen to your poor precious melody —
Like children, play at the things grown ups live,
Anticipating your great days.

## This Fog

If this fog would lift but for a moment,
This fog we live in and are lost in, close-hugging us in pain,
This seething fog, weighted with prejudices, dense
    with the close-packed particles of selfishness,
    crowding vision into blindness,
We would see some strange sights, some wonderful sights —
    so many welcoming smiles,
And we would hear some strange sounds, some wonderful
    sounds — so many welcoming voices; such music!
There would be people greeting one another with all-
    embracing smiles, forgotten smiles, quite guileless.
And there would be great hand-clasps, a majestic look
    in the eyes.
And there would be people falling into one another's
    arms in unimaginable relief.
And there would be eyes brimming over with tears, welling up
    from the depths where profound recognition resides.
And there would be salutations encircling the globe
    like swift, clean breezes, freshening its tired air.
So many old acquaintances, friends, companions, lost
    lovers found.
Ages old, great places, great regions of childhood,
    youth and freedom regained.

Endless reunions attained with but simplicity of vision.
Multitudinous meetings in less than the wink of an eye,
And great home-comings without the least journeying.

## Good Old Earth

Good old earth
Holding the seas
In great hollows —

Tears
In dropped sockets
Held over
And replenishing
Word tired soil —

Soil
Steeped in the vain glories
And long black nights
Of the past dimmed marches
Of men —
To be loaned again
And again —

Given
To the festering-sore process
The screeching sprawling abrasions
The gashes and long blunt wounds
And bleachings to lifelessness
Made by the pilgrimage
Of men —

Men
By mean transformings
Making you habitable
To dark ways
To settlings and seethings and warrings
And the five times down removed
Reflections of magnificence
Splashed in blind pride
Over your long-suffering breast.

Toronto Street, Winter Morning, 1920

Grey Day in Town, 1923

January Thaw, Edge of Town, 1921

Jazz/Billboard, 1921

# III

# PEOPLE

## In the Heart

People do not pass back and forth outside of me.
They do not strut, and loaf, and dance and slink
    along outside of me.
They do not laugh or weep, or curse or pray, quarrel
    or lift loving gazes outside of me.
Nor do they turn from their fellows afraid, and
    ashamed and alone outside of me.
Nor do any that I behold, or think of, live outside of me.
They live in the great heart of me.
There, I welcome them all.
I know the present struggles, and sorrows and joys of each.
I know the not-yet-reached sufferings and tragedies.
And I know the whyfore of these.
I know when, and where, they will stumble and fall
And I know what it is that will make them rise again,
And with tears streaming down their cheeks move on
    once more.
I have lived them through this many times
So that the way will not be strange nor too hard.

## People Sleep

The road runs straight, a ghost laid low;
A line of lights on either side, ending suddenly, breath-
    takingly in the dark.
And behind the lights, in houses, in hotels and above stores
People sleep
On their backs, on their sides, alone and in pairs,
Mouths open, mouths shut, resting quietly, or fretfully turning.
Snoring in a ghastly monotony
Like dead things haunted by incoming and outgoing life.
Heads on arms, knees drawn up,
Or legs thrown wide to a generous angle.
Bed clothes tossed, hair dishevelled.
Gawky, awkward, ugly.
In silly postures, in all postures,
Rid of their trappings.
Honest in the dark, behind drawn blinds,
People sleep.

## Look at All of Us

Here, look at me
Going along my little way —
Here, look at you
Going along yours —
There, look at you-him and you-her,
And me-her and me-him
Going along theirs —
Each knowing what he knows
Or not knowing —
But each
Dragging one foot along
Behind the other
Up hill,
Or down hill,
Or along the gutters —
Look at all of us —
Take a long look.

## Occupied People

So many people
Are busy
Grinding axes
That they never look up
To say
How do you do
With their eyes —
Other people
Exist
Only
To bolster them up —
They do not care
About people
Who will not
Commend them —
'Tis rare
On earth
To be able
To go out
To another,
As if
To say —
Here's you,

Here's me,
Let us smile,
Through and through—
So many people
Are busy
Grinding axes.

## A Question

Are you like that?
Are you sad walking down streets,
Streets hard as steel; cold, repellent, cruel?
Are you sad seeing people there,
Outcast from beauty,
Even afraid of beauty,
Not knowing?

Are you sad when you look down city lanes,
Lanes littered with ashes, boxes, cans, old rags;
Dirty, musty, garbage-reeking lanes
Behind the soot-dripped backs of blunt houses,
Sour yards and slack-sagging fences?

When you see great cities,
Jagged squares of baked clay, and steel and stone,
Canals of filth under every street,
Smoke-breathed, din-shrouded,
Seething with blind, driven people —
Seeing pilgrims settling down in the earth's scum,
In mud,
Feeling swine,
Are you sad?
Are you like that?

## They Never Quite Forget

When people turn a corner,
They look back
From an age-old habit
Of apprehension —
Something tells them
The past waits ahead,
So they look back
To see
If it will smooth away
In the future —
They know.
They never quite forget.

## The Victim

Somebody must be spat upon,
Somebody must be thorn-crowned,
Somebody must be crucified —
Always, there must be a sacrificial victim.

Goaded by greatness
People seek stature in scorn.
Afraid of beauty
The seek safety in defilement.
Driven by fears
They seek courage in killing.

People must belittle themselves,
Spit upon themselves,
Crown themselves with thorns,
Nail themselves to a cross
To find themselves —
Always, there must be a sacrificial victim.

## In the Dark

At earth's midnight
Men mumble in mausoleums —
Way down in the dark
Hard ghosts murmur
About games,
About women,
About religion,
About machines, tools, bonds, stocks, selling points,
    ways and means, booze, babies and bridge, motors,
    meals and taxes, ailments, cures and scandals,
    books, plays and the weather, cosmetics, cooks
    and costumes.
There are directors' meetings, board meetings, meetings
    of creditors, of juries, of deacons, politicians,
    ward-heelers, schemers, thugs and soul-savers.
Meetings of those who curse and those who pray,
Those who deny and those who affirm,
Those who lust and those who hate —
At earth's midnight
Men mumble in mausoleums.

## Finding Sight

People
Cling to the aspiring
And drag them down,
Hold them down,
Bind them,
Crucify them,
Try them out
And find
If they're sound — strong — great.

People,
Blind between birth and death,
Can alone find sight
Through those
Who have been dragged down,
Bound and crucified,
Tried out
And found
Sound — strong — great.

## Earth Life

People,
Drugged by lusts
And plunged into a billion little hells
By self-isolations
Scurry around
Seeking satisfactions —
With voracious earth gaze
They dig the gutters for treasures,
Search gaudiness for pleasures,
Pursue forgetfulness through vices
And fling
Inflictions, revilings, stabs, bouquets,
Loves, hates and fears
On long, short and medium curved
Returning arcs,
That sweep
Through the souls of men
Gathering consequences
And inevitably returning
Home in time
For the harvesting.

## The Hoax

On the shores of time
The lighthouses blink and bow
To sighing-up
And sighing-down ships
As they pass,
And the carelessly tethered beaches run
Along the soft, knife edge of the water,
Undulating muffled, silk greetings.
The winds shift and turn and play,
Howl or whisper
Free over the land,
Free out to sea.
And all the fish,
Wide open eyed in the water,
Perpetually laugh.
And wide opened in light,
The sky laughs
At the people
On the sea
And on the land —
All day long the sky laughs,
And the fish laugh,

And the sea heaves its paunch,
Jostling the ships
At the jest.

## Undaunted

People like front seats at tragedies.
They press around the injured and the captive.
They are curious of freaks and the deformed.
They are irresistibly drawn to hangings and lynchings and
    all brutal spectacles — the sight of blood affects them
    strangely.
Like cattle, dully transfixed, people stare at the scenes of
    tragedies
'Till something stirs inside of them, and they become hungry for
    details.
They crave to know how all phases of suffering and sorrow feel,
    and how it feels to die.
They fear life, so they crave to know about life,
And they fear strangely familiar death.
They fear the appalling stillness of death — the empty, waxen
    cadavers.
People know that all feared things must be met, and dealt with and
    conquered,
So they seek to see themselves on all sides, in all conditions,
    undergoing all experience.
They contemplate their own wounds in the wounded.
They live their own sorrows in the sorrowful.

They see their own fears in the terrified.
They behold their own deaths in the dying.
Everywhere they see themselves, suffering, and sorrowing and
    crucified.
Deep within themselves they know they must down all the dregs
    of misery.
Somehow they know they cannot flee from pain —
That if they do, it will track them down and relentlessly seek
    fulfillment.
So people anticipate their pain,
Live out and discount their pain before it comes,
Ever seeking some secret transmutation.
Something within them knows that in utmost suffering is born
    immortal joy.
That martyrs find a great glory.
That heroism is a divine distillation.
Something within people is undaunted.

## People Are All Right

People are all right.
Every one diddles along,
Or jiggles up and down
On one spot
And never move.

Some make good speeches,
Some mix smooth drinks,
Some play good bridge,
Or drive a long golf ball.
Others carry their liquor well,
Have fine poker faces,
Are good sports.
Some drive swell cars,
Give great parties
Or dress well.

Others make many friends,
Are free and easy.
Some keep up with the times,
Some are well read,
Some play the piano,

Some can sing.
Everyone has his little stunt. —
People are all right.

The righteous
Swell out their chests
With their own wind.
The wicked
Chase around
Stirring up trouble.
Gossips
Dig for dirt
In other people's souls
And pass on the venom.
The timid
Live their lusts
Safely second-handed.
Politicians
Whip old wounds,
Keeping up the angers.
Soul-savers
Save their own souls
Before the gaping public.
The vindictive
See in others

Their own viciousness
And hurt, maim, kill.
The salacious
See in others
Their own lewdness,
And tear, wound, despoil.
The swift sneer at the slow.
The slow censure the swift.
The young look ahead.
The old look back.
Neither see much.
Nobody sees much.
Everybody bumps along
Or up and down. —
People are all right.

Bad eggs smell bad.
Good eggs aren't noticed.
Young men hide dreams
Away under coarse words.
Old men grow sad
When they see the sun set
Children tire of toys,
And so do grown ups.

Rich folks sink into smugness,
Outcasts wander.
Strong folks forge ahead
Weak ones waver.
Mothers weep
When sons go astray.
Girls go wrong,
Wars come along.
The victorious get nothing.
The conquered get nothing.
Nobody gets anything.
Everyone is defeated
But never beaten. —
People are all right.

Men run 'round
Making little fears,
Making little havens,
Making little hells,
Making little heavens.
A breath of wind
And away these go.
But men go on forever.

# IV

# DEFINITIONS

## Familiarity

Hug joy
And it squirms around,
Turns upside down
Showing sorrow.

Loosen the hold
Altogether
And it turns again,
Joy side up.

## Blasphemy

It is blasphemy
To be merely mortal,
To wilt under the weight of the ages,
To succumb to second-hand living,
To mumble old dead catch phrases,
To praise far off ways and things and sneer at your
    neighbour's clumsiness,
To say nay, nay and smile at aspirations, dreams and
    visions.

## Beliefs

Beliefs are belittlements
Held before the soul
Like baubles—
Jingling,
Tingling,
Glitter and tinsel
Dazzling the attention
To agitations
That blind vision
To denials
Of the soul's
All-conquering greatness.

## Might

Might foils itself
In agitation,
Fritters away and is lost
In countless, little beginning squibs,
Little puffs and faint submerged echoes
Let out from puny capacities
In beguiling pride. —
But in calm,
Might mounts
And maintains itself —
Poised in gentle ways,
It hides its severity
In yielding cloaks of tenderness
That shields its fierce capacity
From ruinous descent
Into the sodding abysses
Of lost greatness —
Where the soul
Sucks up gall
To fill its aching emptiness.

## Rhythm

Life rides a rhythm of births and deaths,
Comes into the seen,
Fades into the unseen.
Bodies are born, fill out,
Carry life one step forward,
Shrivel, harden and die.
Nations rise,
Struggle to the top in their vigorous days,
Exult in their full days,
And slip away in their pale days,
Down into murky valleys,
Their songs dying in the dull depths.
Races greet the dawn,
Move forward under the morning sun,
Rejoice at their high noons
And blur out to oblivion in a twilight melancholy.

Lands rise from the sea
Seeking impregnation,
Seeking the sun's light,
Glory in ages of blossom-fragrant springs, harvest-
    weighted autumns,
Become old, worn out, burdened with histories

And sink under the waters once more.
Worlds are born in space,
Circle their orbit,
Spin with ecstasy,
Run down, die, disintegrate —
Rise and fall,
Ebb and flow,
Day and night,
Pain and joy
And the zenith.

## Memory

Memory
Is a feared
Not-letting-go,
A safe clinging
To little assurances,
An old, tired finger of wan hopes
Wagged before exuberance —
And memory
Is a store house
Of thwarted dreams and lost hopes,
Old sorrows and forgotten wounds
That waken,
And murmur
Insistently
When the soul is dragged toward pain —
And memory
Is a handful of slight satisfactions
Thrown over
The one great remembrance
In a frenzied fear
Of greatness.

## Suffering

Suffering
Is being made to look
Against desires —
The weak attention
Forced from its wandering
Into feared seeing —
The gaze,
Pain-sharpened,
To ponder
On one living feeling —
Or the soul,
Having seen some pleasure,
Cannot look away,
But fascinated
Must gaze
Upon the pleasure
Turns to pain
In its eyes —

After the strain,
The pain—
The gaze melts
To a convalescent comfort,
To an easier heart-flow,
Perhaps to kindness.

## Darkness and Light

In the mass darkness is insistent, overpowering.
It presses in so heavily, so smotheringly close.
But taken as a pinch of salt
Between the finger and thumb,
It crumbles;
It can be rubbed away
Losing its coarseness,
Its pressing terror,
Until the thinness
Can no longer hide the dawn-radiance.

Now light
Is just the other way.
It cannot be fingered,
It is so fine.
It must be taken at the flood
When it smoothes through the soul
In a glittering, loved exaltation,
Leaving reflections of beauty,
Leaving warm memories of ecstasy,
Stirring to love-longing the great freedom —
And light has no weight,

Yet one is lifted on its flood,
Swept high,
Running up white-golden light-shafts,
As if one were as weightless as light itself —
All gold and white and light.

## Isolation

Think of the love lavished in cemeteries,
Bathing graves,
And filling the house of the dead
With futile perfumes.
Think of the lives lived in gone loves —
Weepings in great empty spaces
Over bleeding excavations,
The breasts empty,
Panting in sucking sobs
That draw up sorrows
To fill the void.
And think of love frustrations,
Blank wall endings
Throwing back longings
That cram the soul
Into a breaking, crumbling boneyard of dried aches.
And think of the night wailings for a gleam of light,
And the wide-eyed wailings for lust-free sleep.
And the witherings, steel-bound surceases of doubt
Found by the arrogant,
Stumbled into by the weary —

Think of the poverty of lives
Haunting memory for sustaining scraps.

Lost in time
Direction is broken
And scattered,
And the fragments
Sweetened
All separately, alone
In isolation anguish.

### Sadness, Joy and Weariness

Sadness
Can be hugged,
Made much of,
Held warm in the breast
And coddled.
One can drink bitter drops alone,
Unseen,
And from one drop of sorrow
Thinned out preciously
Over days, over years
A life can be made
Saturated in sadness,
Gloom-compressing
The songs in the heart
To aches.

But joy
Has spread wings
Unfolding at ripple-dawns.
Wide-spread soaring wings
Far-pinioned on the light,
Iridescent in noon-sun glitter —

Ecstatic,
Shaking out songs through the day sky,
Youth remembered songs
On the light
To the zenith.

And in the gloom golds
Of evening melancholy
Songs slow away,
Sift to earth surface,
Shrouding the soul
To homesickness
In joy weariness.

## Death

Death
Is not a snuffing out,
Is not a darkness,
Not the great gloom.
It hides no awfulness,
Lurks not grim
Beyond the last breath.

Beyond the rims of radiance
In the little darks,
Dance and strut the hard, faint echoes,
Sway and slink along the soft, faint echoes,
Preening, parading, twisting in and out,
Doing a jig
Before the world mirror.

There are many ideas of death,
Fear born terrors
Of dark blottings-out,
Of empty throat rattlings,
Of open, glassed eyes,
And the stillness beyond —
The silent, engulfing stillness.

But death
Is something lived
In dull mimicry,
A going through meaningless motions
In the midst of life,
Like masses of people
Filling in time
With the inconsequential.

## Time

Time is the womb of melancholy.
Hours move wearily.
Days drag heavy, leaden feet,
Drag them through mires of cloying honey,
Clinging long and sickly sweet.
Nights are weighted to a seeming standstill,
Stop dead almost, in a teeming black void
Where silent wild cries echo, and re-echo,
And return with a wide obliterating slam,
Enfolding into harsh darkness
The soul.

Time flings a million moods through the souls of men,
Leaving dust, leaving sediment—
Old sediments of doubt.
And time pokes a long lean, finger into the souls of men,
Stirring to melancholies, to weaknesses, to hopelessness
Old sediments of doubt.
And time draws a bleary hand over the eyes of men,
Blurring vision into an infinity of slow broken bits.

But when joy fills the souls of men,
Time rides on wings swifter than light.
The hours chase one another like things gone mad,
Days flee from dawn to dark,
Nights blaze past and out,
And then—
Time slows away to a jog trot,
To a shuffling, halting walk
To drabness, endlessness,
Melancholy.

Were there no time
There would be no sadness, no down drag, no melancholy.
One could go back and forth,
And into, and out of,
And be all over at once
Or nowhere—
Find endless ways of escape.
Never being pinned down, held,
Made to taste,
Made to swallow,
Made to linger over every bitterness,
Made to remember so many millions of times,
Just to make sure.

## Suppression

Suppression
Is a holding in
And battening down
Of life
By beliefs —
A forcing of the irrepressible
Into cramped, angular channels,
And swelling these
To billions of hard pressure-pains
That find weak spots,
And leaks are forced
Into little crime jets
That flow away passion-pus
In a temporary surcease.
But stir to responsive quivers
The hidden angers
In millions of men —
And big blood-fountaining jets
Burst forth,
Fiercely free
From cramped life
In the wild orgasm
Of war —

## The Irrepressible

The irrepressible
In its dip into limitation,
Supremely surges through every confine—
Rolls along,
Turning over and over,
And inside out,
And wears to nothingness
All the institutions of men—
It flows away poison ferments
In all the sins,
Drives every sneer to its source,
Sings every song to its conclusion,
Rushes loves and hates to fruition
And plunges lusts to their pain-endings,
Tears loose all fears
From their moorings
To sail the seas of terror.
It plunges into all the hells
And burns them out
And fades out every heaven,
And creates ceaselessly
Through the head,

The hands, the heart, the voice
Of the millions of men,
Fresh molds for its future widening—
Through all time it sweeps,
Creating, breaking and discarding,
Through sins and crimes and catastrophies,
Rebellions, wars and massacres
Inexorable,
All powerful—
A flame that licks along all channels,
Burning everything
Into its own white heat
On its ecstatic return
To freedom.

# V

# SPIRITUAL

## Breath

The soul shrinks in sorrow
And expands in joy
Breathing itself
To a God-like capacity.

## The Hours

The hours go by
Travelling through time
On one another's heels,
Gathering their harvests
Of love and hate,
Lust and loftiness.

And the hours wait
Just beyond the coming minute,
At the end of time
For the purging
And loosening back
Into free space.

## The Battlefield

When one takes hold of life
The heavens cloud and darken—
In the distance rumbles the approach of a great storm,
And under the far, high pilings of solemn and awful clouds
Legions of beings from most remote places,
And from near places,
Draw together
For the great battle—
For ages they may assemble
All in the soul
And one can do nothing.

## Weaving the Future

The exodus of the ages
Gathers up its train
From the far dim past,
And the near past,
And unfurls it
Ahead again
Continually —
Spreading the past
Into the future,
Through the blind indifference,
Or the bleak despair,
Or the cleansing vision
Of you and me.

## Illusion

I walk out into the night
To face the unknown terrors,
And at the first blast from the dark, I falter,
And would fall back, pampering my weakness—
Fool—the overarching gloom is not in the night.
The night does not teem with dread things,
'Tis your own shuddering soul that is full of the black,
Shrouded in drapes—veils
Blotting out light,
Making murk where there was none,
Making night,
Making terrors,
Making all the misery of men.
Fashioned from a handful of space—
From nothing.

## The Beast

Shame spreads thin
Over a crowd
And gets lost.

In numbers,
The beast finds its might.
Maddened by greatness
It roars in a mob,
Hounds its prey,
Tears flesh,
Spills blood,
Breaks bones,
Never touching greatness.

It takes lightness
To rise above the mass,
A loss of all coarseness,
A smoothness of soul,
So that the beast
Has nothing to cling to.

## Unseen Tears

Do you know how beautiful are unseen tears?
How much more distinct and familiar and lovely than seen tears?
Have you never felt them behind faces, raining down,
Behind gracious faces, strong gentle faces;
Faces suffused with an august sadness —
The outermost, faint rim of radiance from their falling?
Tears soft and soothing as the cool of silent evenings,
Mightier than the flooding light of the noonday sun,
Diamond clear — clearer than the high waters of mountain lake —
Distilled from wondrous wounds,
Exquisitely refined,
And all healing to the wounds from whence they came.
O, translucent, teeming veil of tears,
Too effulgent for the eyes of men,
Beyond men — deep within man,
What unimaginable glories you hide!
Even to apprehend the mists that rise from your falling
Is to become enchanted —
A lover
Of the sure, far off, golden dawn of majestic life.

## *The World Doubts*

The whole world doubts
And flaunts its doubts —

Streaking over the earth
Throughout time
Go all the countless, fear-grown doubts,
Lashing and slashing,
Shifting, weaving and criss-crossing
And mixing
To grim greys and dirty drabs,
And clotting to dark blots
Black-shadowing the earth —

Millions of men
Are blurred, blotted out,
Lost in the confusion —
Now and then
Some lover of light,
With living vision,
Pierces a way
Through the smudgy, weaving womb —

Loosening,
Letting down
Long shafts of golden ecstasy
On millions of mire-bowed heads —
But few raise their heads.

## No Music

So long as any rancour
Flushes the soul a dull red or hard, poison green,
Or any belief isolates the soul
To a false security,
Or it stands
On the faults of others
To gain stature,
There can be no love of men, no freedom —
No music
Ethereal, celestial, majestic,
Can surge through
Sweeping away age-old clinging dregs,
Old clotted pains and doubts,
And dusting
The dim memory-haunted corners
Of old dry joys,
Still dwelling sweet —
No music
Quickening into gold-singing flame
All heart homesickness
'Till darkness burns out,

Leaving the soul
Transparent,
Full-receptive
To all radiance.

## The Sea Wind

The wind blows in from the sea
Over the grim, gaunt hills across the bay,
And over the moored boats in the harbour,
Stirring all things.

A great voice is the wind from the sea,
Resonant over all the seas' horizons,
Teeming with the mighty murmurings of remote and
     forgotten majesties,
Yet closer, nearer the heart of man than the world of these
     days —
The steel and sweat and grime of these days,
The hard-edged blocks of buildings, jutting from the ground
     in stifling clusters,
The rattling, humming, life plundering rhythm of a billion
     machines,
Tall sooty chimneys, black smoke, poison fumes and mad,
     intensified fires,
Beauty parlours, dance halls, movie houses, slaughter
     houses — all sorts of bawdy houses,
And paper flooding the world with the bawlings in print of
     those with wares to sell —

A ceaseless grasping, an orgy of diversions,
Lost are the lofty ways of those who give.

The wind blows in from the sea.
Such a soul-stirring voice is the wind from the sea,
Resounding in deepest memories, and quickening these with
    its strong, sweet, melting pains,
Calling into present days and drowning their little
    notes in its ampler, fuller voice —
Majestic voice, alive with the murmur of many bygone,
    golden ages —
Wondrous, lost golden ages,
Slumbering beyond the far horizons,
Quietly waiting their radiant resurrections,
When on their endless journey,
Men again become great.

## The Earth Winds

The earth is such a pale thing in space,
So drab a bleached grey —
There are purer, richer, more translucent colours
In the heart.

There is little hope outwards,
Just an endlessness of diversions,
Littlenesses everywhere to pin down the attention —
Inexhaustable littlenesses,
Breaking off infinitesimal bits from the mind.

Over the earth's scum
Evanescent, fading out mind-bits,
Paling to old tawny ashen-bleached greys —
The life breath sucked out
By the sun.

Rattle of shells,
And dried out buff husks,
And swirling old dead leaves —
The whispering swish of sucked out, dried and dead things
Sighing,
Waving futile, pale hands,
Swaying arms,
Pleading-void
In the earth winds.

In people
There is a sun,
A centre of light, of hope.
A rose of bliss
Forever fragrant,
Sweet Jesus-breathed,
So still,
Lost in the husks,
Deep swirl-hidden under dead leaves,
Ages upon ages of dry ashen leaves
Blown dead by the earth winds.

Winds of hate,
Winds of lust,
Winds of doubt and wantonness—
Great crucifying gusts
Tearing over the earth's surface day and night,
Ripping jagged, bleeding-crimson
The heart of man—
Sweet Jesus-breathed heart
Forever fragrant
In the husks.

## Great Song

Down through the ages
Goes great song
Quickening the dead.

We forget that it is we ourselves who make all conventions,
rules and prohibitions. We forget that adventure is the joy of life,
or perchance we grow too weary for effort.

When we curb life we curb art, and when we curb art we curb life.

We live only when we adventure and give expression to the results
of our adventure. We should understand then and never forget that
we permit all rules, conventions, institutions and prohibitions to
become stable only that we may thereby have a base from which
to adventure further.... And we should recognize and never forget
that all pioneering is the advance guard of our adventure into
the unknown where greater and greater amplitude of life awaits us.
And we should further know that any pioneer in any pursuit
is going to discover something new, untoward, strange and perhaps
unpleasantto our grooved ways of life and to the exact extent
in which he does so is he of value to us.

— LAWREN HARRIS, from the *Notebooks*

The Gas Works, 1911–1912

Morning, 1921

Italian Store in the Ward, 1922

Building the Icehouse, c.1916

# AROUND THE WARD

*The Relics of Lawren Harris' Toronto*

In the small of Toronto between the two great wars of the twentieth century, Lawren Harris walked these city streets with an eye for the beauty and spirit behind the surface doldrums of Hogtown's various forms of poverty. The city was much smaller then, claustrophobic even, and Harris got caught up in a social scandal that forced him to leave not just the town, but the country as well. He eventually returned to Canada from the American desert – but to Vancouver – a much changed artist, having fully embraced the mystical values he was only just discovering in Toronto. This tour revisits Harris' days in the city when he too walked these streets, trying to navigate and resist its puritanical and closed-society values and hierarchies. He was also, however, trying to build up an alternative set of values that might lead his society forward into a better future culture. He was not alone as a mystic in the city, nor as a visionary with grand hopes and an avant-garde harkening for what it may become.

There is nothing left of the Ward: once a thriving if impoverished neighbourhood, it was erased by city planning with the construction of College Park (1930), the Hospital for Sick Children (1951), the New City Hall (1965), amongst other large-scale projects in the area. The neighbourhood survives in spirit in Kensington Market, but there is little to see or feel of the Ward as it was, where it was, in Harris' time. In contrast, his early modern world survives with official city sanction, tucked between the markers of progress of a condo-crazy city. Harris' daily world formed a stone and brick arc wrapped around what was once the Ward. The following guide revisits the relics of his Toronto, reimagining the milieu that led him to step outside his customary comfort, to step into the mystery of the Ward.

> *"Harris is Canada's only important revolutionary painter."*
> —NORTHROP FRYE, 1948.

## DAVENPORT AND BATHURST: THE HILLCREST COMPLEX AND WYCHWOOD PARK

If you walk from Christie Street east down Davenport Road, you will notice the stately TTC Hillcrest complex. Giant husks of cast-aside buses and trolleys and streetcars grow rusty in the failed fields behind, guarded by two rows of chain-link fences, sleek tube-like cameras, and a guard's booth befitting a prison. The rattling gates open and close throughout the day, sealing shut the hermetic space of a metallic cemetery and its secret dead. The complex was built to hail the dawn of the modern public transit era – and the end of the small horse-drawn streetcar operations that ran from Front Street. The whole complex disappears into the curve of hill, discouraging memories or reminiscences or even wistfulness. The city changed, that's all – if you choose to look, you can find the stretch-mark scars of its progress. The classic Toronto red-brick façade, opened in 1924, shows no signs of age or wear, and is still of functional use to the city, despite the endless horizon of wrecks.

You can see, but hardly notice, the humble gates across the street of Wychwood Park, the transformed estate of Marmaduke Matthews' abandoned Arts and Crafts revolution in 1888. He was a rich man with money from his toil as an official painter for the CPR, and invested it all in this potentially perfect society based on the writings and inspiration of William Morris, the British socialist poet, book-maker, furniture and wallpaper designer. (A short walk away at the corner of Bloor and Avenue Road, in the back offices of the neo-classical Department of Household Sciences Building hangs one of Morris' original great stain-glassed windows – closed to customers by the present owners, the once-Canadian Club Monaco.) Marmaduke Matthews bought the land on the cusp of the hill, took it out of the public domain, and, working with the renowned architect Eden Smith, built a network of roads and houses for his artist colony. The imagist poet Louis Moray Bowman lived at 3 Wychwood Park (later the home of Marshall McLuhan (Geddes 387)). The area is still a private enclave, rustic and forested, disappearing from the road's eye.

The brown waters of Taddle Creek ran through the community, though its currents have since been dammed into a painterly pond, fenced-off like a treasured artwork from unwanted visitors. It has become a kind of fetish in the contemporary city: a handful of magazines, schools, and stores about town bear its name, and non-members of the Wychwood Park private, gated community often sneak in to paint the city pond and forest dwellings. As Shawn Micallef notes in his book *Stroll*, the pond by the gates is the only place where the old and buried Taddle Creek is still visible. It is worth a moment to wander this parklike neighbourhood, that still, to this day, controls and regulates its own infrastructure.

## DAVENPORT AND SPADINA: CASA LOMA AND THE BALDWIN STEPS

Continuing down Davenport, you pass Casa Loma, the great edifice that ruined the far-sighted man who built it, and the ostentatious Baldwin Steps. Spadina Road (not the Avenue) was once, by the Baldwin family, hoped to be the central and spectacular *rue de grâce* of the city, though that dream too slipped away. They built the steps to make it happen. But there was no one big enough to fight to finish their vision; essentially no one to pay for it, to pull it into being against the stone weight of inertia. The poor called the road Spa-die-na, the rich Spa-dee-na – which is how the stately (and state-funded) museum atop the stairs is still pronounced. Even as the ramshackle brick houses are rapidly being consumed by the new wealth of the city, the democratic impulses of the city won out and we all say Spa-die-na now. From the top of the switchback stairs, you can see the glitter-flicker of Lake Ontario with, as Harris describes, "its strong, sweet, melting pains."

Davenport passes Poplar Plains Road, the namesake of the city in Bertram Brooker's 1936 novel, *Think of the Earth*. Brooker won the country's first Governor General's Award for Literature for the book. Brooker remains renowned primarily as a painter – like Harris, a mystical modernist painter from the Toronto 1920s. Harris, in fact, organized the first exhibition of Brooker's work in 1927, the same year Emily Carr and the international avant-garde came to visit. Brooker's one-man show was first, though, and stands as the country's first exhibition of abstract painting. At the launch of Brooker's abstracts, Harris opted not to give a speech, not to say anything though Brooker had hoped for some public embrace. The audience was clearly put off by his show, and Harris chose to play it safe. By that point in the year, it would have been generally known that Harris was funding a massive exhibition of avant-garde European and American art in Toronto – the first showing of the work of Kandinsky, Schwitters, Dali, Man Ray, and many more – a few months later. The *real* avant-garde. Brooker left his first show crushed and dejected and forlorn (see Roald Nasgaard (22-23) and Brooker's diary entry from 24 January 1927 for more on the exhibition and the incident described).

In turn, the protagonist of Brooker's acclaimed novel has many loose resemblances to Harris. The character is a mystic who looks to the mountains, the Canadian mountains, as the icon of northern spiritual intensity and purity, as a metaphor for the spiritual impulse in his mind: "The vastness and height of the imagined scene had become mingled with the loftiness of his aspirations. He believed that there, at the foot of some towering peak, the final inspiration – the high impulse he had so long awaited – might come to him." In a teasing, perhaps mocking, gesture, the character turns out to be a maniac lost in mystical delusions. Brooker's relationship with Harris resembles a friendly rivalry with a rich undercurrent of bitterness. In notes to an unfinished novel from 1925, Brooker provides a character sketch of Manchee, who will be "Something like Harris." The description Brooker provides gives some insight into what he thought of his friend and peer:

Supremely confident of his art and rather self-centred, rather wanting to be courtiered, especially in his own studio.... As artist a revolutionist.... As a Canadian almost ferociously patriotic, with a great feeling for the country.... As a mystic he also believed that things are going to happen in this country, indeed are happening. He feels himself in the vanguard of the movement and is looking for every sign. Unless people show some sign of it he is impatient with them.

At the time, Harris lived on Cottingham Street which intersects with Poplar Plains Road. Brooker lived at 107 Glenview Ave, farther up Yonge, but walked Poplar Plains to access the secret bohemian heart of the city veiled in Wychwood, in Casa Loma, and in the Group of Seven's Studio Building on the other side of Yonge. Toronto was not a city of cafés or public squares. Worse, alcohol and even dancing were strictly controlled. Writers and painters and musicians and other members of the libertine class thus took their drinks in private parlours, in private clubs, in speakeasies, in secret society meetings. Casa Loma, after its original owner died, became one such venue for dancing and drinking and listening to modern music. But outsiders visiting during the period, like Ernest Hemingway and Wyndham Lewis and Aleister Crowley and W.B. Yeats, were shocked to find that there was *no place to go* in Toronto, no downtown scene where diverse crowds of literati gathered and sparred or provoked misfit adventures. None of those visitors stayed very long. It was true: everything of any note happened behind closed doors, hush-hushed, — or worse, happened up in Muskoka on private cottage estates with small bugs and an even more tightly controlled audience. Brooker, for his part, wrote articles calling for the "opening up" of Canadian society; encouraged Canadians to "wake up" and try harder ("When We Awake!" 17). In the 1930s, he went on a lecture tour across Ontario and Quebec encouraging Canadians to be more eccentric in public, to dress more vivaciously, and sing while promenading down main streets. The women from the Heliconian Club applauded his efforts and invited him to afternoon tea. The Orangemen struck him from their list of toastmasters. Critics called him "eccentric."

Eccentrism was, however, in the air during the period. By the late '20s, Harris had become the most prominent member of the increasingly prominent Canadian Theosophical Society, an openly occultist organization. He led workshops and gave lectures on art and mysticism. He was warm to Brooker's notion of Canadians leading a spiritual revolution, but Brooker's explosive and colourful geometric paintings must have challenged Harris more than he would publicly admit. Though he said nothing about them, within five years, he began painting notably similar geometric abstractions of his own. By 1934, upon leaving Toronto, he stopped producing realist landscape art altogether. The Group of Seven, though an important stage in the development of art in the country, was no longer radical enough to justify. Brooker, for his part, turned his abstract paintings into abstract plays into abstract poems into strange novels. In the eyes of many – particularly the mystical class – he replaced Harris as the

leading modernist of the times. To drive home the point, according to the *Hamilton Spectator*, Brooker's work was "a sign of Canada's coming-of-age in the field of art."

Just up the road, the house at 212 Poplar Plains was designed by Eden Smith, the architect of Wychwood Park and Lawren Harris' iconic Studio Building.

## DAVENPORT AND YONGE: THE MASONIC TEMPLE AND THE STUDIO BUILDING

As Davenport turns south and crosses Dupont, it curves all the way over to Yonge and becomes a poignant reminder of the city's penchant for amnesia. Everything is new and far distant from the hard life that was once eked out in this neighbourhood. Yorkville, which blossomed later, has itself been co-opted by the same financial power that it once reacted against: Hollywood and Hemingway and massively expensive art not for the people. Occasionally, Group of Seven paintings that were once traded for food and lodgings are sold here at prices only Lawren Harris' wealthy industrial family could have afforded. Now, there are dozens such families in the city, but none so idealistic. At the corner of Davenport and Yonge, the Masonic Temple after thousands of initiation rites and ritualized semi-occultist services has been transformed in the new Toronto into a television studio for MTV.

You cross Yonge Street, where horses once worked, and you are just a short distance from the Studio Building, now tucked behind a Canadian Tire, on the edge of Rosedale. Though the artists' workshop sits literally on the other side of the tracks, the decidedly *tonier* side, it is likely the painters would have crossed over to lunch and dine in the cafés and restaurants and clubs of Yonge. The Arts and Letters Club, for instance, a "comradely haven for kindred souls," is just a short walk away, down near College. Such benevolent aristocracy as Wilfrid Laurier and Vincent Massey used the club, and all the Group of Seven (not to mention Bertram Brooker – and Ernest Hemingway) were members. Eden Smith designed the gorgeous interior fireplace. J.E.H. MacDonald served many years on the club's executive, including as President for two. According to A.J. Casson, the members of the Group and their like-minded tribe would gather at the Club "everyday for company and a good meal." Though essentially genteel, the Club allowed its prim feathers to be occasionally ruffled: it was at the club in January of 1927 that Brooker held his provocative exhibition of abstract art.

The Studio Building, itself, boasts a classic Toronto design: sharp red brick with unglamorous warehouse style. It has large windows that span floor to ceiling on the front face of each of its cathedral floors. It stands alone and anachronistic on Severn Street, on the edge of the Rosedale Valley, bordered by a small parkette and subway tracks behind. The small stand of grass and bush and oak that wrap around the stately structure has since been named after Lawren Harris – the city's only public memory of the man. This building was also designed by Eden Smith, the great architect of Wychwood Park. It is still in use as an artist studio, and still in good repair.

During the winters of 1914 to 1916, the legendary guide to the Canadian wilderness Tom Thomson lived in a shed out back (a building that has since been moved to the grounds of the McMichael Canadian Art Collection in Kleinberg), cursing the pretensions of the art world. In summer, Thomson went back to his canoe and Algonquin Park, where he died in 1917. In 1927, Emily Carr walked wide-eyed in this workspace listening to modern music and allowing herself to slip into the trance of Lawren Harris' ruminations on art, nation, and spirituality. She was utterly transformed: "Oh, God, what have I seen? Where have I been? Something has spoken to the very soul of me, wonderful, mighty, not of this world. Chords way down in my being have been touched" (25). The members of the Group were the first to embrace her as a most serious artist; Lawren Harris the first to see the soaring spirit in her work.

o o o

The Studio Building also became the centre of the public scandal that forced Harris out of the country. Two regular visitors to the only house on Severn Street were Fred and Bess Housser, a young married bohemian couple whose lives fell apart in 1934. Fred Housser had become involved with the artist, teacher, and prominent social figure Yvonne McKague. Bess turned to the also-married Lawren Harris for help, who offered her a temporary room in the Studio Building. This public indiscretion was too much for the small of Toronto and social pressure mounted for a return to propriety and decorum. To be clear, Bess and Lawren were spiritual partners, but not lovers. The optics of the situation, however, led many to conclude otherwise. Enflaming things, the parents of Lawren's jilted wife Beatrice Phillips (known as Trixie) began threatening to press charges of bigamy if the matter was not solved quickly. The whole community was up in arms, and nobody, it seems, questioned Fred for his role in the mess. Society united against Bess and Lawren (for more on the scandal see Larisey 117-119).

Bess would later remember appealing to a friend and being angrily told to leave the premises. A.Y. Jackson and Bertram

Brooker sided with Fred Housser, who had taken, conveniently, to blaming his own infidelity on Bess and Lawren's relationship. Bess, as she wrote in a letter in 1934, was forced to confront the "social usage" of scandal: of people – *artists!* – jockeying for some vaguely conceived illusion of power. They had chosen their team, unaware that, after Harris left, the Toronto modernist initiative would essentially and quickly vanish: that history would barely remember those Harris left behind. Bess and Lawren, fed up, frustrated, and hurt, left Canada in July, for New Hampshire and then eventually the American desert. In the meantime, in the thick of the scandal, Lawren discovered something rare and precious. He was already married, but he and Bess found in each other the great potential filled and never separated until her death in September of 1969. He passed away just four months after her.

She and Fred divorced in 1934 in *absentia*. She had already slipped down to Reno, Nevada, with Lawren – where he, too, divorced his wife. They fled, ultimately to New Mexico to join a bohemian collection of modernist mystical painters from around the world led by the celebrated and eccentric American painter Agnes Pelton. Inspired by everything from Zen Buddhism to Dynamic Symmetry, they explored spiritualized abstract art under a collective name, the Transcendental Painting Group (1938-1942). For Bess, the desert must have felt free and timeless after the moody agitation of her former home.

When Emily Carr learned of the Lawren and Bess affair she sniffed in her private journal: "None of my business but I feel somehow as if my connection in the East were over" (215).

Fred Housser died in 1936. His funeral brought out a large and sympathetic crowd; in fact, it became a significant if distressing gathering of Toronto's artistic community. Bertram Brooker read the eulogy and served as pallbearer. Lawren and Bess, still painting mystical visions in New Mexico, did not attend. Though he died only two years after Bess had left, Fred Housser had already remarried. Bess sent the widow a compassionate note; the two eventually became affectionate companions through correspondence (Larisey 119).

Portrait, Beth Housser, c.1920

Unlike Bess, Harris was not leaving an unfaithful spouse. He left Trixie, his wife of twenty-four years, and their three children. He left behind countless friends, a custom-designed Art-Deco mansion, and any and all commitment to the Toronto mystical modernist community – but not to mysticism or modernism in general. In fact, the break from leading Toronto's modernists (and apparently giving the reins over to Brooker) allowed him to act on significant lifestyle changes he had been working towards for a while. They were all of a similar nature – he finally and formally left the Christian church for theosophical mysticism, he stopped painting representational landscapes (urban and wilderness) for non-representational abstracts, and, with Bess, he gave up a conventional Canadian marriage for an unconventional mystical spiritual union.

Ironically, though they had been publicly excoriated for adultery, Bess and Lawren's love affair and marriage was not physical or sexual. They kept separate bedrooms in New Hampshire, in New Mexico, and, eventually, when they returned to Canada, in Vancouver. The scandalous and seemingly salacious marriage which had cost him so much was never consummated. In their theosophical composite of eastern beliefs, it was thought that to combine moral restraints (*yamas*) like celibacy with moral observances (*niyamas*) like the worship of God would re-awaken the "third-eye" with its untold psychic and occultist power: it was the key to achieving *chelaship*, essentially theosophical enlightenment. As H.P. Blavatsky, the founder of the Theosophical Society wrote, "[N]o one can properly or with safety enter on the study of Practical Occultism, in the real sense of the word, unless he or she is a celibate" (612-3). For this reason, for the mystical potential and fulfillment he discovered with Bess and their theosophical practice, Lawren Harris, the wealthiest artist in the Dominion, perhaps the Commonwealth, who had grown up with every opportunity and material delight, found resolution and power in going without. They left the urban decay of Toronto to consume itself and set off hoping to, as Lawren Harris wrote in an unsent letter in 1939, "achieve real spiritual oneness with all of life."

## Elm and Yonge:
## the Arts and Letters Club,
## the Ward,
## Nathan Phillips Square and
## Chestnut Street

Down Yonge Street you pass the former home of the Theosophical Society in Canada at 52 Isabella Street. Continue down to Elm Street where the Arts and Letters Club dwells in a world unto itself – lush wood panelling, old whiskey, and a rich archives overloaded with uncatalogued files and fonds with one hundred years of collections; whimsy and bromide combined. Paintings fill all of the walls to the corners. Lunch, as ever, is served at noon, buffet style. Beer and bombast included.

Upon arriving at this mecca of modernist Toronto, the arc we have completed across the contemporary city's midriff provides a frame of what was once the poorest neighbourhood, a hurdy-gurdy place resplendent with picturesque poverty. Lawren Harris' bohemian world encircled and contained this world. Massive civic projects, like the TTC Hillcrest complex, Toronto General Hospital, and the old City Hall grounds just to the south were consciously designed to erase the ghetto in the core; to push them out. The neighbourhood, in fact, shifted west and established what we now call Kensington Market across Spadina (Spa-die-na). At the time, the wealth and pomposity of the Club stood in stark contrast to the Ward, its contextual neighbourhood. The overworked horses, the crumbling stucco homes, and the weary pedestrians on their infinite tread have since been replaced by designer carpeting and gourmet Italian and the new City Hall. The Eaton Manufacturing Building was but one casualty of progress. The condos in this area are now like castles, with prices that sound like Gross Domestic Products. During and between the wars, however, workers walked these streets to the munitions and farm equipment factories owned by Harris' family. They trudged back exhausted and drained in the evening. The roads were mud, the houses crooked and sun-baked. There were thieves and bums and evangelists blocking easy passage. Even the parks were littered with garbage and spoiled love affairs. Yonge Street was a confusion of bleating cars, horses, and streetcars. Gawkers stood idly by, smoking cigarettes or stepping over horseshit to get into pool halls. Peddlers pushed their wares, plundered the scrap heaps for treasure.

o     o     o

In an anonymous article called "Life in the Ward" from 1915 (City of Toronto Archives), one writer described the ethnic neighbourhood in the following way:

> The district that lies between College and Queen Streets, Yonge Street and University Avenue is generally regarded by the respectable citizens of Toronto as a strange and fearful place into which it is unwise to enter even in daylight, which after dark no sane person would dream of running such a risk! The danger that lurks in these crowded streets is not always clearly formulated in the minds of those who fear it, perhaps it is the dagger of an Italian desperado of which they dream – perhaps the bearded faces of the "Sheenies" are sufficient in themselves to inspire terror – but at any rate the fear remains and probably it could best be analyzed as Fear of the Unknown.

A few years later, in a report by the Bureau of Municipal Research called "What is 'The Ward' Going to Do with Toronto?", the agency authors reached a more psychological conclusion:

Properly speaking, 'the Ward' is a condition, an attitude of mind toward life, a standard of living – not merely a geographical locality …. not only is the inhabited part of 'the Ward' becoming more congested, but it is 'boiling over' into adjacent areas and new 'Wards' are springing up sporadically in other parts of the city as a result of the same economic and social forces which produced the parent 'Ward.'

The report proceeds to paint a fairly gruesome portrait of an urban ghetto:

In roughcast houses, plaster has fallen off, and there is, more or less, an absence of paint or whitewash. Fences about the houses have partly collapsed and no effort is made to repair them or to remove them altogether. Sidewalks leading to the houses and doorsteps are in a broken condition, and the doors themselves are usually in a state of ill-repair. Wooden shutters sag from one hinge or have many slats missing …. Rags and unused clothing lie scattered about, mingled with broken pieces of furniture, tin cans, broken stovepipe, and other junk, without any danger of being disturbed by the residents.

The comfortable, colourful decrepitude insulted Toronto the Good. Not Harris though; he set about painting, walking, hearing, and listening to the wild space outside the clubhouse door. He brought his sketchbook and his notebook; painting and writing as he went. He was not listening or searching for specific individuals: he wanted to capture the meaning and experience of life there *in general*.

Walking those mud-strewn and dishevelled streets in the predominantly Jewish neighbourhood, though, it must have occurred to him that his family employed many of those whose ramshackle homes he was painting, and whose toils were certainly a source of the profits that enabled his luxurious upbringing and his art. After he left Toronto, he never painted urban life again. The hardship and the decay in these paintings are all we get of the Ward, even despite the now nostalgically remembered lively culture of the neighbourhood. It was recorded, for instance, that bands of young men in the Ward, young Italian men, would walk the streets with instruments and sing into the night; that aging Jewish mothers would scold their children in Yiddish arias; that, unlike in the rest of the city, life was lived in the streets, in the open. To credit Harris' awareness of this unique urban space, it has been noticed by many that – like the red door of his poem – the colours of the buildings have a rhythm, a gaiety, and a dance; like a secretive soulful smile into the weariness of the wasteland. Even these paintings leave the impression of time and space being reconciled for a moment in the splash of colour on canvas.

To finish the tour, carry on to Chestnut Street tucked behind the great parenthesis of the new City Hall. Shadowed and dense, and vibrant with public life, the city barely resembles, barely remembers the cloistered quiet of Lawren Harris' Chestnut Street. Workers once lived here, passed here en route to the factories, such as the Eaton's factory, those owned by the Harris family, and the Gas Works nearby. All of this world is gone now, washed over by the city. Harris, however, captured for us a small slice of the world he discovered, in his search for more.

# Works Cited

Baily, Samuel L. *Immigrants in the Lands of Promise: Italians in Buenos Aires and New York City, 1870-1914*. Ithaca: Cornell UP, 1999.

Blavatsky, H.P. *The Esoteric Papers of Madame Blavatsky*. New York: Kessinger, 2005.

Brooker, Bertram. Diary. 24 January 1927. University of Manitoba Special Collections. Box 1 Folder 16.

——. "When We Awake!: A General Introduction." *Yearbook of the Arts in Canada 1928-1929*. Toronto: Macmillan, 1929. 3-17.

Carr, Emily. *Hundreds and Thousands: The Journals of Emily Carr*. Ed. Gerta Moray. Toronto: Douglas & McIntyre, 2006.

Frye, Northrop. *Northrop Frye on Canada*. Ed. Jean O'Grady and David Staines. Toronto: University of Toronto Press, 2003.

——. "The Pursuit of Form." *Canadian Art*. 6.2 (Christmas 1948). 54-57.

Harris, Lawren. *Notebook 1922-1925*. Libraries and Archives Canada. Lawren Harris Fonds.

Larisey, Peter. *Light for a Cold Land: Lawren Harris' Work and Life – An Interpretation*. Toronto: Dundurn Press, 1993.

Micallef, Shawn. *Stroll: Psychogeographic Walking Tours of Toronto*. Toronto: Coach House, 2012.

Powell, John. *The Encyclopedia of North American Immigration*. New York: Facts on File, 2005.

Shacks, 1919

Old Houses, Toronto, Winter, 1919

Toronto, Old Houses, 1912

Red House, Winter, c.1925

# Further Readings

LAWREN HARRIS AND THE GROUP OF SEVEN:

King, James. *Inward Journey: The Life of Lawren Harris*. Toronto: Thomas Allen, 2012.

Murray, Joan and Lawren Harris. *Lawren Harris: An Introduction to His Life and Art*. Toronto: Firefly Books, 2003.

——. *The Beginning of Vision: The Drawings of Lawren S. Harris*. Toronto: Douglas & MacIntyre, 1982.

Reid, Dennis. *Atma Buddhi Manas: The Later Work of Lawren S. Harris*. Toronto: Art Gallery of Ontario, 1985.

Silcox, David. *The Group of Seven and Tom Thomson*. Toronto: Firefly Books, 2011.

ON TORONTO AND THE WARD:

Agocs, C. *Ethnic Settlement in a Metropolitan Area: A Typology of Communities*. Ethnicity. 8: 127-148. 1981

Caulfield, J. *City Form and Everyday Life: Toronto's Gentrification and Critical Social Practice*. Toronto: University of Toronto Press, 1994.

Harney, R. "The Immigrant City." *If One Were to Write a History*. Eds. P. Ancitil and B. Ramirez. Toronto: Multicultural History Society of Ontario, 1991. 173-182.

——. "Ethnicity and Neighbourhoods." Ed. G.A. Stelter. *Cities and Urbanization: Canadian Historical Perspectives*. Toronto: Copp Clark Pitman, 1990. 225-245.

——. *Italians in Canada*. Toronto: Multicultural History Society of Ontario. 1978.

Harris, Amy Lavender. *Imagining Toronto*. Toronto: Mansfield Press, 2010.

Hayes, Derek. *Historical Atlas of Toronto*. Toronto: Douglas & MacIntyre, 2009.

Hiebert, D. "Jewish Immigrants and the Garment Industry of Toronto, 1901-1931: A Case Study of Ethnic and Class Relations." *Annals of the Association of American Geographers*, 83 (1993). 243-271.

Kluckner, Michael. *Toronto the Way It Was*. Toronto: Whitecap Books, 1988.

Piva, Michael J. *The Condition of the Working Class in Toronto, 1900-1921*. Ottawa: University of Ottawa Press, 1979.

Speisman, Stephen A. *The Jews of Toronto: A History to 1937*. Toronto: McClelland and Stewart, 1987.

Tulchinsky, G. *The Origins of the Canadian Jewish Community*. Toronto: Lester Publishing, 1992.

Zucchi, J. 1988. *Italians of Toronto: Development of a National Identity, 1875-1935*. Kingston and Montreal: McGill-Queen's University Press.

OTHER TORONTO WALKS:

Carlson, Neil. *City Walks: Toronto: 50 Adventures on Foot*. Toronto: Chronicle Books, 2008.

Micallef, Shawn and Marlena Zuber. *Stroll: Psychogeographic Walking Tours of Toronto*. Toronto: Coach House Books, 2010.

Seymour, Murray. *Toronto's Ravines: Walking the Hidden Country*. Toronto: Boston Mills Press, 2000.

# Questions for Discussion

1. Why is Lawren Harris concerned that the inhabitants of the Ward are "outcast from beauty"?
2. Northrop Frye calls Harris a "revolutionary painter." Revolution means leading a great change in society. What kinds of things would Harris change in Canada?
3. The introduction argues that the poems "populate" the empty city depicted in the paintings. Who do we get to meet in the Ward? Why has Harris chosen to focus on these individuals?
4. The introduction also argues that Harris tries to incorporate ugliness into his style of writing because of his subject. What other things does he incorporate into his style?

ABOUT THE POETRY, *CONTRASTS*

I ~ DESCRIPTIVE

1. "A Note of Colour." What does it mean that someone has painted their door "a bright gay red"?
2. "In a Tea Room." What is the significance of the different directions of the women's gazes?
3. "The Evangelist." The Evangelist seems to juxtapose the street scene. Why?
4. "Morning and Evening." What happens to the people between the morning and the evening that leaves them so changed?
5. "The Harbour." Does the harbour or the sea offer any respite from the industry of the city? How does this contrast with other depictions you know of water?

6. "Little Houses." Which painting does this poem best pair with?

7. "Greetings." Explain why the speaker thinks he has been understood when the dialogue suggests otherwise.

8. "Picnic Grounds." How is the whole earth like this "old, stale, picnic ground"? Would you characterize this as an environmentalist poem?

9. "Overlooking the Sea." This is another poem in which Harris challenges the poetic habit of romanticizing the sea. This isn't a critique of industry though; what point is he making against the water here?

10. "City Heat." This poem, which has been internationally anthologized, captures the modernist sense of urban crisis and distrust of progress. How do the various metaphors in the poem contribute to this impression?


## II ~ EMOTIONAL

1. "You and I, Friend." What do you think is beneath the "mask" and "disguise" the speaker would discard?

2. "After War." What kinds of things associated with war does Harris avoid in this poem? How do you account for his decision to not talk about them?

3. "Who are You?" What do we know about the person addressed in this poem?

4. "Drops of Pain." What does the speaker hope to find in the drop of pain that is in "every pleasure"?

5. "The Age." Is Harris' description of his age still true? How have things changed?

6. "What a World!" What is the tone of this poem? How does the speaker feel about the "mad, seething cargo"?

7. "Pity the Vindictive." Why should we pity the vindictive?

8. "Good Fellows." What are the problems of alcohol according to this poem?

9. "Keep Moving." Change is constant, according to this poem. Looking back on the negativism of the previous poems, do you think the speaker might take some comfort in thinking that nothing in the world is permanent?

10. "Rehearsal." This poem speaks out against fakery and "false greatness." What marks these "self-elected martyrs" as different from the "grown-ups" the speaker prefers?
11. "This Fog." This poem uses a metaphysical conceit. What does the fog represent?
12. "Good Old Earth." There is only one period in this entire poem, making the whole one great sentence. How does this grammar relate to the theme of the poem?

III ~ PEOPLE

1. "In the Heart." What impact does the use of anaphora have in this poem? Note the transition in repeated pronouns from the beginning to the end of the poem.
2. "People Sleep." What is the key phrase in the poem that reveals the speaker's attitude to all the sleeping people?
3. "Look at All of Us." This poem makes a game of pronouns. What do you learn by taking a long look at all of them?
4. "Occupied People." The lines in this poem are very short and choppy, as if distracted and annoyed. What is the speaker annoyed at?
5. "A Question." This poem includes a number of lists. What kinds of things does the speaker list? What impact does the list format have on the topics described?
6. "They Never Quite Forget." What waits ahead of people in the future?
7. "The Victim." Why must there always be a victim?
8. "In the Dark." This poem contains a remarkable contrast in styles between the abstract imagery at the start and the stark, specific images in the two long lists. Map out the relationship between these two elements of the poem.
9. "Finding Sight." Identify and discuss the shift that occurs between the two stanzas.

10. "Earth Life." What returns home in time for the harvesting?
11. "The Hoax." Who laughs in this poem? Why are they laughing?
12. "Undaunted." What are some contemporary examples of the voyeurism Harris describes? What remains undaunted in humanity?
13. "People Are All Right." A lot of the previous poems have addressed negative dimensions of modernity in Canada and in the world. How does this poem challenge or modify the implications of the previous poems?


## IV ~ DEFINITIONS

1. "Familiarity." What familiar aphorisms does this poem call to mind?
2. "Blasphemy." This poem, however, declares it a blasphemy (an offence against God or sacred things) to speak with aphorisms and clichés. In what way could such speech acts be considered blasphemous? What would that imply about human language?
3. "Beliefs." How is the speaker's notion of the soul's "All-conquering greatness" different from the beliefs he belittles?
4. "Might." This poem revolves around a pun, using multiple meanings of the word "might." Reread the poem with this duality in mind and explain how it changes the meaning.
5. "Rhythm." What is the perspective of the speaker in this poem?
6. "Memory." According to the speaker, what might we give up if we stopped "clinging" to memory?
7. "Suffering." What happens after the strain, the pain of "being made to look"? What is being looked at? What do you think it looks like?
8. "Darkness and Light." This poem, like many of the others, works through a juxtaposition. Compare and contrast the central metaphors in the juxtaposition.
9. "Isolation." This poem might be a useful opportunity to revisit some of the details of Harris' biography and some of the personal suffering he experienced

while writing these poems. What does this poem suggest about the speaker's experience of loss?

10. "Sadness, Joy and Weariness." Instead of the usual binary, this poem establishes a ternary of abstract nouns as its central theme. How does the speaker relate each of these elements to one another? Do the metaphors for each assist in this relationship or make it more complicated?

11. "Death." What is death to the speaker? What is it not?

12. "Time." The speaker images existence without time. What would that be like? What kind of things would change?

13. "Suppression." The speaker connects suppression to the ideology of society. How do our beliefs suppress us? What ultimately becomes of this repression?

14. "The Irrepressible." Read this poem as a possible answer to all the negativism of the poems in the previous section, including the negative depiction of the sun in "City Heat." In what way is this poem optimistic?

## V ~ SPIRITUAL

1. "Breath." The speaker creates a complicated metaphor of the soul as lungs. Explain how the metaphor works.

2. "The Hours." What type of figurative language does Harris use in this poem to characterize The Hours? What happens to them after their work?

3. "The Battlefield." Where does this battle take place?

4. "Weaving the Future." What becomes of "you and me" in this vision of the future?

5. "Illusion." What does the speaker make in the night? What are these things made of?

6. "The Beast." What is the beast and why is it dangerous? Where have you encountered this beast?

7. "Unseen Tears." Where do the unseen tears come from? Why do they not fall?

8. "The World Doubts." What do people doubt that black-shadows the earth?

9. "No Music." What prevents the "majestic" music the speaker yearns for? What kind of music (or musical experience) is he talking about?
10. "The Sea Wind." How is the sea characterized in this poem? How does it contrast with the other poems about the sea in the book?
11. "The Earth Winds." The speaker identifies a negative and a positive sun in this poem. What is the difference between the two?
12. "Great Song." What is the great song and how does it quicken the dead? Compare and contrast the music in this poem with "No Music." In what way does this poem serve as an appropriate conclusion?


GENERAL EXERCISE

The five canons of rhetoric was a common subject covered in everyone's schooling in Lawren Harris' time. These five canons of rhetoric were developed by the ancient Greeks, and principally by the great Roman thinker Cicero, and include:
- invention (to find the subject),
- arrangement (to organize into arguments),
- style (to choose a way of speaking),
- memory (to argue by recalling things),
- and delivery (to pronounce one's argument).

That Lawren Harris' book is also structured into five sections (or canons) merits a comparison between the two. In what way do each of the sections of Harris' book correspond to the five canons of classical rhetoric? Are there any specific poems that connect to this structure?

What other systems of five elements can you think of (hint: think of Elizabethan theatre)? How do these other systems compare with *Contrasts*?

# The Paintings:
# A Complete Listing

In the Ward, 1920
Oil on canvas
86.7 x 92.7 cm
In the collection of the University of Manitoba
Winnipeg, Manitoba, Canada

The Eaton Manufacturing Building, 1911
Oil on canvas
76.2 x 75 cm
Private Collection

Hurdy-Gurdy, 1913
Oil on canvas
75.8 x 86.6 cm
Art Gallery of Hamilton
Hamilton, Ontario, Canada

Houses, Chestnut Street, 1919
Oil on canvas
81.7 x 97.2 cm
The Robert McLaughlin Gallery
Oshawa, Ontario, Canada

Toronto Street, Winter Morning, 1920
Oil on canvas
97.5 x 112.2 cm
National Gallery of Canada (no. 5010)
Ottawa, Ontario, Canada

Grey Day in Town, 1923
Oil on Canvas
82 x 97.7 cm
Art Gallery of Hamilton
Hamilton, Ontario, Canada

January Thaw, Edge of Town, 1921
Oil on canvas
107 x 127.2 cm
National Gallery of Canada (no. 5005)
Ottawa, Ontario, Canada

Jazz/Billboard, 1921
Oil on Canvas
108 x 127.6 cm
Private Collection

The Gas Works, 1911-1912
Oil on canvas
58.6 x 56.4 cm
Art Gallery of Ontario
Toronto, Ontario, Canada

Morning, 1921
Oil on canvas
97.2 x 112.4
Foundation of Beaverbrook Art Gallery
Fredericton, New Brunswick, Canada

Italian Store in the Ward, 1922
Oil on canvas
81.8 x 97.2 cm
National Gallery of Canada (no. 5012)
Ottawa, Ontario, Canada

Building the Ice House, 1916
Oil on canvas
26.7 x 32.4 cm
Private Collection

Portrait (Beth Housser), c.1920
Oil on Canvas
112.5 x 92.5 cm
Art Gallery of Ontario
Toronto, Ontario, Canada

Shacks, 1919
oil on canvas
107.9 x 128 cm
National Gallery of Canada (no. 1693)
Ottawa, Ontario, Canada

Old Houses, Toronto, Winter, 1919
Oil on canvas
82.5 x 98.1 cm
(unknown location)

Toronto, Old Houses, 1912
Oil on canvas
38.1 x 38.1 cm
Private Collection

Red House, Winter, c. 1925
Oil on canvas
84.5 x 97.5 cm
Hart House Permanent Collection
University of Toronto
Toronto, Ontario, Canada

an Exile Editions Graphic Poetry book

*www.ExileEditions.com*